Who Needs a REEF?

A Coral Reef Ecosystem

KAREN PATKAU

TUNDRA BOOKS

Copyright © 2014 by Karen Patkau

Published in Canada by Tundra Books, a division of Random House of Canada,
One Toronto Street, Suite 300, Toronto, Ontario M5C 2V6

Published in the United States by Tundra Books of Northern New York,
P.O. Box 1030, Plattsburgh, New York 12901

Library of Congress Control Number: 2013943892

Library and Archives Canada Cataloguing in Publication

Patkau, Karen, author
        Who needs a reef? : a coral reef ecosystem / by Karen Patkau.

(Ecosystem series)
Ages 7-10.
Issued in print and electronic formats.
ISBN 978-1-77049-390-2 (bound). – ISBN 978-1-77049-391-9 (epub)

        1. Coral reef ecology – Juvenile literature. I. Title. II. Series:
Patkau, Karen. Ecosystem series.

QH541.5.C7P38 2014   j577.7'89   C2013-904506-6
                                                  C2013-904507-4

Edited by Sue Tate
Designed by Karen Patkau
The artwork in this book was digitally rendered.

www.tundrabooks.com

Printed and bound in China

1 2 3 4 5 6   19 18 17 16 15 14

To Dr. Jane Berg,

with special thanks to my family and friends.

WELCOME TO THE REEF

Near a tropical coast, where the sun beats down and the salty sea is shallow and warm, an underwater jungle grows.

Schools of brightly colored fish swim through a garden of corals and sponges. Razor-toothed barracudas lurk nearby.

Above sea fans and sea grasses, a stingray sails. A father seahorse hangs on to seaweed. He carries over a thousand eggs in his pouch.

How beautiful and strange the reef is, bustling and teeming with life!

INSIDE A CORAL POLYP

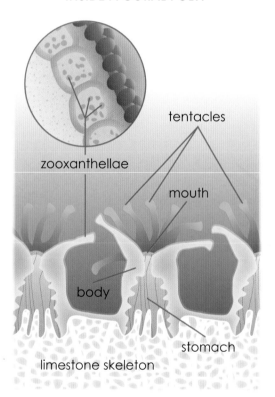

tentacles

zooxanthellae

mouth

body

stomach

limestone skeleton

HOW A CORAL REEF FORMS

The colorful, coral reef surface covers a massive, stony-white structure. It is made from the skeletons of millions of tiny animals called coral polyps.

A live polyp secretes calcium carbonate, a substance it gets from seawater. A hard limestone skeleton forms, which surrounds and protects its soft body.

Zooxanthellae live within the polyps' bodies. These plantlike organisms give corals their rainbow of colors.

Over centuries, layers of polyps build up, becoming the reef's base. A colony of polyps is able to build a vast castle for itself and other reef inhabitants.

LIVING ON THE REEF

There are more kinds of living things on coral reefs than anywhere else in the sea. Each one has a purpose that links it to others in its underwater environment.

A coral reef is an ecosystem. Let's meet more of this one's plants and animals.

Coralline algae coat parts of the reef and help cement it together. Sea anemones and sea squirts also attach themselves to it. They look more like plants than animals.

"*Crunch, crunch, crunch.*" A parrotfish munches on the algae-covered coral. Sea snails graze on it, too.

There are many types of hard corals, such as elkhorn, giant brain, sheet, and finger coral.

In a nook in the reef rests a green moray eel. A triggerfish pokes at a starfish that is prying open a clam. An angelfish swims gracefully by.

Dolphins surf in the waves. A large group of sergeant major damselfish swim together. There is safety in numbers against big predators.

Like most fish, a Nassau grouper sucks in oxygen-rich water to breathe. His gills absorb the oxygen, then pump carbon dioxide-loaded water out of his body.

A porcupinefish sees a nurse shark.
He inflates himself by gulping water.
Hopefully, he will appear too big and
prickly to be swallowed!

At night, hungry creatures emerge from their daytime shelters. Those out during the day now hide in the reef's crevices, where they sleep.

A swimming crab flees yellowtail snappers. A spotted cleaner shrimp waves her antennae, while an octopus scuttles over the reef.

Plankton are tiny life-forms that float in the water all the time. They are food for coral polyps, moon jellies, and many others.

Watch out for sea urchins on the sandy bottom! Their sharp spines are poisonous.

THE FOOD CHAIN

All living things need energy from food to survive. Energy passes from one living thing to another to another. This process is called a food chain.

The reef food chain starts with tiny plants, or phytoplankton. Like land plants, they make their own food using water, nutrients, carbon dioxide, and the sun's energy. To get the most sunlight, they grow near the sea's surface.

Zooplankton are tiny animals. They feed on phytoplankton. Many small sea creatures feed on both types of plankton.

In a food chain, larger animals usually eat smaller ones. Amazingly, a huge whale shark eats mainly tiny plankton!

PLANKTON

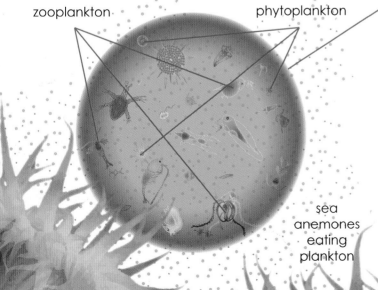

zooplankton

phytoplankton

sea anemones eating plankton

BACTERIA

LIFE IS A CYCLE

All plants and animals die eventually. In the sea, their uneaten remains sink to the bottom, to be used by other living things.

A sea cucumber is a scavenger, feeding on leftover bits on the sea floor. A hermit crab crosses the reef, carrying her seashell home on her back.

Bacteria live on and decompose dead matter. They break it down into simpler substances, including nutrients that they release into the water.

Sea currents carry nutrients up to plankton, which need them for nourishment … and the cycle starts again.

THE REEF PROTECTS THE SHORELINE

Waves are ripples and ridges that move across the water's surface. Winds, storms, and even earthquakes cause them.

The reef protects nearby land from erosion by reducing the force of powerful waves that crash into its seaward edges.

Waves that could smash into the shoreline, washing away sand, plants, and soil, are slowed down. Then gentler waves roll over the reef toward land.

A healthy reef slowly grows back and repairs the damage caused by waves. It takes a very long time for it to recover from a violent storm.

BEACHES AND HARBORS DEVELOP

By protecting the shoreline, a coral reef helps develop natural harbors and beaches.

A natural harbor is the part of a body of water that is shielded by land from rough waves. Boats can safely anchor here.

A beach is a strip of shoreline, covered by sand or gravel. It develops as particles of coral, rock, seashells, and coralline algae are washed onto the shore.

Sea turtles come ashore to nest and lay their eggs in the sand.

THE REEF IS PRODUCTIVE

The reef is bountiful. It provides a rich harvest of food for sea creatures and for people living on nearby land, where soil may be poor for farming.

Many species on the coral reef produce valuable substances used in science and medicine.

A substance from sea sponges called psammaplin A is used to treat certain types of cancer.

Tourists come to enjoy warm sunny weather, sandy beaches, and amazing reef wildlife, adding to the local economy.

WHO NEEDS A REEF?

Changes in weather have happened naturally throughout Earth's history. Varying temperatures and ocean currents can make seawater too hot or too cold for reefs to survive.

Human activities cause greenhouse gases to be released into the air, adding to global warming. Phytoplankton absorb and reduce the amount of some of these gases, such as carbon dioxide.

Overfishing, catching tropical fish for aquariums, collecting coral, or walking on a reef harms it. Pollution also threatens reef health.

In the tropics, logging and farming cause soil to wash down rivers and into the sea. This muddy water smothers coral and blocks the sunlight algae need to thrive.

If the coral dies, reef animals and plants lose food and shelter. They will disappear, too.

Who needs a reef? We all do.

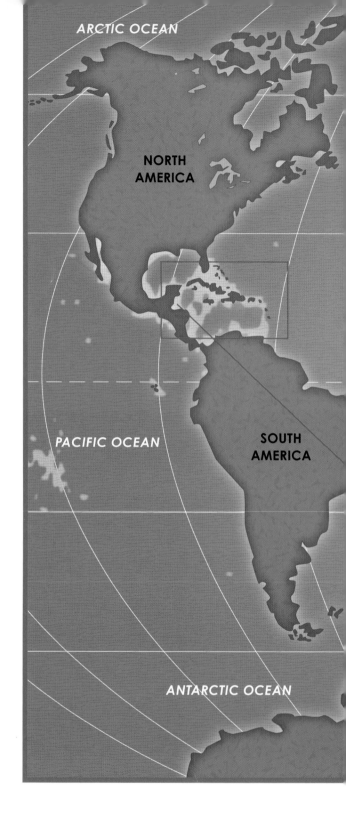

ARCTIC OCEAN

NORTH AMERICA

PACIFIC OCEAN

SOUTH AMERICA

ANTARCTIC OCEAN

CORAL REEF AREAS OF THE WORLD

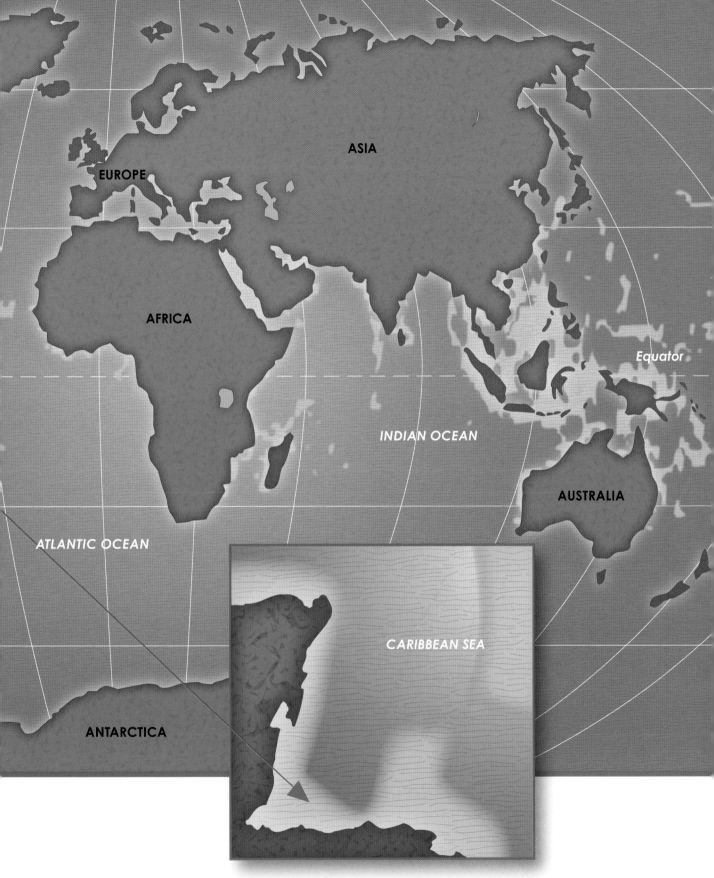

The reef described in this book is in the Caribbean Sea off Central America.

HERE IS MORE INFORMATION ABOUT SOME OF THE REEF INHABITANTS:

Clam
The clam has an upper and a lower shell to protect its soft body. A muscular hinge connects the two shells, allowing the clam to open and close them.

Coralline Algae
These algae contain calcium carbonate. They form a strong crust on rocks and coral. Coralline algae are one of the building blocks of a coral reef.

Dolphin
One of Earth's most intelligent animals, the dolphin is a fast swimmer and deep diver. It is known for its acrobatics, leaping out of the water into midair.

Elkhorn Coral
Named for its likeness to elk antlers, this large branching coral is one of the most important reef-developers. It grows tall and covers large areas.

Green Moray Eel
A long snakelike fish, this green eel has smooth scaleless skin. Although its long sharp teeth sink deeply into anything it grasps, it is more shy than fierce.

Hermit Crab
Because its soft abdomen does not have a hard covering, the hermit crab moves into an empty seashell for protection. As it grows, it must find a larger shell.

Moon Jellies

Made mostly of water, moon jellies have round, clear, jellylike bodies without brains, hearts, and blood. They use stinging cells for self-defense and catching prey.

Nurse Shark

This large shark eats bottom-dwelling sea life. The mother shark gives birth to twenty or thirty pups. All sharks have skeletons of tough, elastic tissue called cartilage.

Octopus

The eight-armed octopus travels by jet propulsion. It changes color and texture for camouflage. Squirting a cloud of black ink into the water, it escapes predators.

Parrotfish

Its front teeth packed together to form a parrotlike beak, this fish scrapes algae from coral and rocks. After digestion, it excretes sandy particles, which help create beaches and islands.

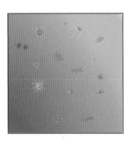

Phytoplankton

Most phytoplankton are single-celled plants, growing near the sea's surface. Other types include blue-green algae and protists. Tiny living things, protists have both plant and animal qualities.

Sea Anemone

Rippling tentacles encircle the mouth of the sea anemone, set atop its short, thick trunk. The tentacles search the surrounding water and pull food into the sea anemone's mouth.

Sea Cucumber

This animal has a soft, cucumber-shaped body. Like an earthworm, it breaks down organic matter into food for bacteria, which recycle it into the environment.

Sea Fan

The sea fan is a fan-shaped colony of soft corals with flexible skeletons. The colony faces water currents, filtering out tiny particles of food that wash through it.

Sea Grasses

These marine plants have small flowers, long narrow leaves, and grow in coastal areas, often in large underwater beds, or "meadows." Turtle grass is a common type.

Seahorse

The female seahorse lays her eggs into the male's pouch – the only animal on Earth to do this. Once the eggs hatch, tiny baby seahorses are released into the water.

Sea Turtle

This large marine turtle has a bony or leathery shell. It swims effortlessly with its four paddle-shaped limbs. Adult males have long tails, while females have short ones.

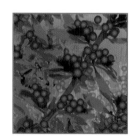

Seaweed

Seaweed is a multi-celled alga. Gas-filled sacs keep some kinds from sinking too deep. It is farmed in water and harvested throughout the world for food.

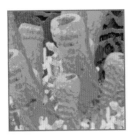

Sponges
Sponges are invertebrate animals that fasten themselves to one place. They rely on water flowing through their bodies for food particles, oxygen, and to remove wastes.

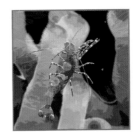

Spotted Cleaner Shrimp
The spotted cleaner shrimp lives on a sea anemone. Waving its antennae, it attracts fish to clean. It eats parasites and algae off of the fish's body.

Starfish
Most starfish have five arms growing out of a central disk. Their mouths are on their undersides. They like to eat slow-moving animals, such as clams, oysters, and snails.

Whale Shark
The sea's largest fish, this gentle giant swims near the water's surface. It scoops up plankton and small fish with its huge mouth and strains the water out through its gills.

Zooplankton
Zooplankton are tiny marine creatures that include single-celled animals, little crustaceans, and very young animals. For protection, they can have transparent bodies, stingers, or a bad taste.

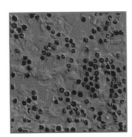

Zooxanthellae
These single-celled algae, living within a coral polyp's body, sop up the polyp's carbon dioxide waste and give off oxygen that the polyp breathes.

GLOSSARY

bacteria – tiny single-celled organisms that break down the remains of other living things

camouflage – a disguise that makes something appear as part of its surroundings

currents – areas of water or air flowing in a certain direction

ecosystem – a community of plants, animals, and organisms that interact with each other and their physical environment. There are many different ecosystems on Earth.

environment – the surroundings and conditions in which something exists or lives

erosion – the process of wearing away rock or soil by the action of wind, water, or ice

global warming – the rise in average temperature of air near the earth's surface since the mid-twentieth century

greenhouse gases – gases in the earth's atmosphere that trap heat. The main greenhouse gases are carbon dioxide, methane, and nitrous oxide.

inhabitants – living things that dwell in a certain place for a period of time

invertebrate – having no spine

nourishment – food or nutrients necessary for health, sustenance, and growth of a living thing

nutrients – substances that give nourishment to a living thing

organisms – living things

pollution – the contamination of the environment by impure substances from man-made waste

predators – animals that hunt other animals for food

prey – an animal that is hunted by another animal for food

scavenger – an animal that feeds on leftover food or plant and animal remains

seawater – water in oceans and seas that contains salt

secretes – produces and releases a substance

tropics – warm, humid regions around the middle of the earth